BLACKJACK
"PLAYING TO WIN"
BY
TONY KORFMAN
HUMOROUS AND INFORMATIVE GAMING GUIDE

TO MICHELLE — MY INSPIRATION

Printing history:
First printing, May 1985
Second printing, November 1985
Third printing, May 1986
Fourth printing, August, 1986
Fifth printing, March 1987
Sixth printing, September 1987

Copyright © 1985 by Tony Korfman.

All Rights Reserved. No part of this book may be reproduced i
any form without the permission of the author under penalty c
intense pain.

This book is purely informational. It is not intended to incit
gambling or rioting. It is not to be used against a husband c
wife in a court of law.

Book Cover by Joe Thomasula. Thanks Joe. you did good!

Published and Distributed by Gaming Books International, 151
East Fremont Street, Las Vegas, Nevada 89101
Printed by American Printing, Las Vegas, Nevada, U.S.A.

Library of Congress Cataloging in Publication Data

Korfman, Tony, 1942-
  Blackjack: a humorous and informative gaming guide.
(Playing to win)
  1. Blackjack (Game). I. Title. II. Series: Korfman, Tony, 1942-
Playing to win
GV1295.B55K67 1985   795.4'2   86-4797
ISBN 0-934047-02-2 (pbk.)

TABLE OF CONTENTS

INTRODUCTION

"The thrill of victory and the agony of defeat." These are feelings that are felt not only by World Series or Super Bowl winners. Many of us know the feeling of riding home in our car with no money in our pockets after visiting Reno, Tahoe, Vegas or Atlantic City for a night or two. "But the next time will be a different story," you mutter. With the help of this booklet it **could** be a different story.

I have been watching customers gambling their money for over 20 years and everything is written from experience. The entire "Playing to Win" series is designed with you in mind. We will be discussing how to play, and above all, "playing to win." I wish you health, happiness and the best of luck on your next gambling venture. Have fun.

Tony Korfman
Author

QUESTIONS - QUESTIONS - QUESTIONS

Everyone enjoys quizzes, especially when a school grade is not dependent on them, so I thought it would be a good idea for you to take a "quick quiz" before you read this booklet. Read and answer the questions as if you were betting $1 and then answer them as if you were betting $1,000. When you finish reading the booklet then take the quiz again. The answers are in the back of the book - just like they were in the "old days." Peek if you want. See if I care.

1) If the dealer has a 7 showing, would you hit a 6 and an ace if your bet is $1_____? $1,000_____?

2) You are dealt two aces and the dealer has a 10 showing. Would you split the aces if your bet is $1_____? $1,000_____?

3) The dealer deals a hand and you notice all the fives are dealt during the course of that hand. Does that excite you?_____ Would you a) Increase, b) Decrease, or c) Keep the same bet for your next wager, if the dealer doesn't shuffle? Would you hug the dealer if you won the next hand?

4) Which 21 game offers the best advantage for you as a player? a) Single Deck_____ b) Double Deck_____ c) Shoe (4 decks or more)_____ d) Shoe Box (20 decks or more)_____ e) Shoe Store_____

5) If the dealer has a 6 showing and you are dealt two sevens, would you split the 7's if your bet is $1_____? $1,000_____?

6) Would you "double down" (double your bet and receive one card face down) on 10 or 11 if the dealer has a 6 showing and your bet is $1_____? $1,000_____?

7) The dealer has a 6 showing and you are dealt two 10's. Would you split the 10's if your bet is $1_____? $1,000_____?

8) You are dealt a 12. Everyone "knows" that if you hit a 12 you bust. The dealer has a 7 showing. Do you hit if your bet is $1_____? $1,000_____?

9) You are dealt a Blackjack (any 10 or face card and an ace) and the dealer has an ace up. The dealer asks if you want insurance and your Allstate broker is nowhere in sight to advise you. Do you take insurance if your bet is $1_____? $1,000_____?

10) The dealer has a 5 showing. You are dealt a 10 and a 2 for a total of 12. Do you double down (double your bet and receive one card face down) if your bet is $1_____? $1,000_____? Do you double down if you're betting the money the guy in the office gave you to bet for him?_____

11) The dealer has 5 or 6 showing and you are dealt an ace and a 2. Do you double down if your bet is $1_____? $1,000_____?

12) Would you hit a 12 if the dealer has a 4 showing and your bet is $1_____? $1,000_____?

13) You are dealt two 5's. The dealer has a 7 showing. Do you a) Split the 5's, b) Double down with the 5's, c) Just hit the 5's.

14) You walk up to a 21 Table with no players and hand the dealer a $20 bill for change. The dealer shakes her head and sighs deeply. Right away you feel uncomfortable. You should a) Tell the dealer the funniest joke you've ever heard. b) Jab the dealer in the eye with your thumb using moderate pressure and a downward motion. c) Spill your drink and **really** get the dealer pissed. d) Find another dealer that is more friendly but not before you blow your nose and leave the Kleenex on the table.

15) You are dealt a face card and a 7 and the dealer has a 10 showing. Do you hit if your bet is $1_____? $1,000_____?

16) You should always order the best alcohol the casino has to offer and above all, drink rapidly since it's free. TRUE_____FALSE_____

17) Dealers make between $50,000 and $75,000 a year. TRUE_____FALSE_____

18) If you are a reasonably good player (bets vary between $5 and $25 every hand) you should try to establish a rapport with a pit boss. TRUE_____FALSE_____

19) You have won $2,000 playing 21 and you're overjoyed as you walk to your hotel room. You should make one stop before you go to your room. Which is it? a) Casino Cashier. b) Security c) Hotel Desk. d) Rest Room. e) Craps Table. f) Keno. g) The blonde at the bar.

20) The "Playing to Win" series includes books on a) Poker, b) Blackjack, c) Craps, d) Slots, e) Keno, f) Roulette, g) Needlepoint.

21) I will write Tony Korfman (the author) a thank you letter when I win playing Blackjack. TRUE_____FALSE_____. To extend my gratitude I will send him a portion of my winnings not to exceed: a) 10% b) 20% c) 50% d) I think he deserves all my winnings, f) Tony who?

ABOUT THE GAME

The origin of Blackjack is unknown. I could make up some complicated story with all kinds of "window dressing" and evolve it from the days of Caesar (not to be confused with Caesars Palace) but it would just take up space and be pure unadulterated bull. The game is still evolving and still in a state of change.

In the past twenty years, more has been learned about the game than in all the years since it was born. As you read this book you may see terms or words that are not totally familiar to you. Refer to the Glossary in the back of the book if you feel the term is not explained to your satisfaction in the text. All the terms that are most common in the Gaming Industry should be in the Glossary. If there's one missing, I'm sorry.

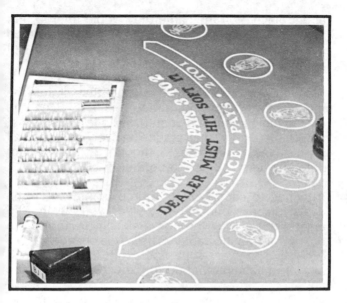

BLACKJACK BASICS

THE TABLE— Blackjack, or "21" as it is frequently called, is played on a table with 6 or 7 chairs to accomodate 6 or 7 players. The table is semi-circular in shape, and on the layout there are 6 or 7 circles or squares for these 6 or 7 players to bet in. Each player bets in the circle or square that corresponds with his seat. The dealer stands behind the check rack. (Chips are called checks in the industry. I should say, chips that have a specific value embossed on them, are called checks or you might think I've gone off the deep end already and think Lay's really makes Potato Checks.)

The cards are dealt from left to right and the first player position on the dealer's left is called first base. The position on the dealer's right is called third base. If you could hear pit personnel converse about players on the game they would refer to first base, third base, the guy **next** to first base, the broad next to third base, or the kid in the middle. I'm not making this stuff up - these are true-isms.

Most tables have a small plaque that states the minimum and maximum bet and any rules the casino feels should be posted. I was in a casino last month that had a small plaque on every game and all it said was, "welcome." I thought it was kind of cute. (I guess you had to be there.)

Attached to each table is a drop box in which the dealer places your currency when you buy-in. She inserts the money through a slot in the top of the box, with a plastic paddle. The box is changed at the beginning of every shift. Each shift is 8 hours long except in casinos that do not stay open 24 hours a day.

THE PIT — In most casinos the various type games are grouped in formations, and in each of these formations, is the area known as the "PIT." If a casino only has one Roulette table and one Craps table, they enjoy the company of the Blackjack tables and the formation is laid out in such a way, that there is one common pit area. This is done so that pit supervisors can observe **all** the games with relative ease, and less supervisory personnel are needed.

THE PERSONNEL — In the Blackjack or 21 Pit, the chain of command is Dealer, Floorman or Pit Boss, Shift Manager and Casino Manager. Larger casinos have a distinction between Floorman and Pit Boss, while smaller casinos use them interchangeably since they are usually the same person. A Shift Manager is in charge of all the games on his shift in all the pits, and the Casino Manager is responsible for the entire casino. I haven't forgotten the dealer.

The dealer is the workhorse. She, and I say she because most of the casinos are leaning toward women Blackjack dealers, usually goes to a Blackjack school for 6 to 8 weeks to become proficient in her craft. It costs from $300 to $600 depending on the school she attends and there is no job guarantee. When she graduates from dealer's school she is considered a break-in dealer and serves her apprenticeship in a casino that will hire break-ins. Her pay starts at $28 for an 8 hour shift and in casinos that do hire break-ins, the tips or tokes are in the neighborhood of $15 to $25 per day. She can expect to gross around $1,000 a month with the hope and expectation of someday being accepted at a casino in which dealers enjoy much larger tokes.

How the tokes are divided is policy that is set by the individual casinos, but in no casino that I know of is a dealer allowed to keep the tokes she herself made on her table. They are pooled and divided equally amongst all the blackjack dealers. Here is where the policy varies. In some casinos the tokes are divided amongst the Blackjack dealers on each shift, and in others they're divided on a 24 hour basis, whereas all the Blackjack dealers working that day are included in the pool. This method seems to reduce the probability of "hustling" by any individual dealer, since they have to split the money "hustled" with so many other dealers.

Hustling is defined in many ways in the Gaming Industry. Some casino bosses think that a dealer saying "Good Luck" to a player is hustling. To me, that borders on sheer ignorance. Friendly dealers are an asset to any casino. My definition of a "hustle" is when a dealer specifically asks a player to make a bet for her. Friendly conversation and developing a rapport with customers can only mean repeat business for a casino. There are many arguments against friendly dealers but I don't agree with them. Meanwhile, back to our break-in Blackjack dealer.

On a typical day she works 8 hours with a break every 40 minutes, 45 minutes, or 1 hour depending on casino policy. The break is either 15 minutes or 20 minutes and most casinos have a break room or break area for the dealers. They usually are eligible for a paid medical plan after their probationary period and have paid vacations after 1 year of employment. It's a good career for women that have no expertise in any specific field, if they can tolerate standing in one spot for up to an hour at a time and dealing with all types of people. One Pit Boss told me there are so many women dealers in the pit now, he gets sympathetic menstrual pains every month. A 25 year old girl with a new Mercedes and a diamond ring the size of my poodle, once told me that all a girl needs in this industry, is a pretty face and a trick pelvis. I guess she had both.

THE PLAYERS — Players come from all walks of life and from all parts of the country and the world. Each player at the table is playing against the dealer. It's hard to believe, but it doesn't matter how bad someone plays at the table; it doesn't affect the long term outcome of the hand. I say long term because you will run into situations occasionally in which the bad decision of one player to hit a hand they should have stayed on will upset the other players. This happens especially when the player takes the card that would have "busted" the dealer. But that player could have equally taken a card that would have **made** the dealer's hand. Even though people get upset at novice players that don't play exactly the way they do, it means nothing percentage-wise. And that's what counts — the percentage against you. The important thing is for **YOU** to play correctly and consistently at all times. Don't worry about the other guy's play. If it bothers you that much, change tables.

THE BUY-IN — When you walk up to a Blackjack table, read the plaque on the table and this should tell you what the minimum bet for that table is. If it doesn't, ask the dealer. If it meets your requirements, then proceed to give the dealer your money by setting it down next to the circle or square and say "change please." **DO NOT** put your money inside the circle or square, as this is the betting area in which you will make your bets.

When you are learning the game, you should start with minimum bets until you are familiar with not only the game, but the strategies involved in playing it. This book will take you through all the phases of the game, but initially you may just want to get the "feel" of playing. If this is the first time you are playing, the excitement of the experience should be enough of a thrill for you without worrying about betting strategies. After a few sessions of betting the minimum, you should be comfortable enough to apply betting techniques. Hopefully, you will apply everything you read, the first time you play, but this is unrealistic. Don't be shy about tearing out the Blackjack Roadmap, which tells you how to play every hand, and having it in front of you when you play. What the hell, it's **your** money!

THE CHECKS — "Chips" are called "Checks" in the Gaming Industry. They are usually in denominations of $1, $5, $25, and $100, and are arranged neatly in the rack in front of the dealer. The largest denominations are located in the center of the rack, with smaller denominations located in the outside tubes. The $5, $25, and $100 checks are always divided by a dollar check so that the table inventory can be counted with ease. Most casinos religiously keep track of their $25 and $100 checks at all times.

Bear in mind that you can buy-in for more checks at any time, and when you do, you will receive just checks. The dealer has no currency, so if you have a hundred dollar bill and want $20 in checks, you can either accept the $100 in checks and put $80 in your pocket or purse to cash in at the casino cashier at a later time, or get up and go to the casino cashier and get the hundred dollar bill broken down. Checks of every denomination cost the casino about 30¢ each, so if you choose to put the $80 in checks in your pocket or purse, don't forget to cash them in. If it's souvenirs you want, go to the gift shop or ask for a casino matchbook with their logo on it. Checks are very expensive souvenir items by comparison.

When you are done playing and want to cash your checks in, you have to take them to the casino cashier for redemption in cash. The dealer doesn't have any currency available to her, so she cannot cash them in. She can however "change color" for you, and this means she will take your checks and give you larger denomination checks, so they are easier for you to carry. If you have a problem because you have stacks and stacks of the largest denomination checks and you want to cash in, the Pit Boss will supply you with a rack. That's a problem every player would like to have.

THE CARDS — The deck or decks used in a game are standard 52-card decks. They are typically "Bee" playing cards manufactured by the U.S. Playing Card Company and usually have the casino logo imprinted on each card. Casinos contract U. S. Playing Card Company for 50,000 to 100,000 decks at a time and pay between 95¢ and $1 a deck, as of this writing, (February 20th, 1985,

2:30 a.m.). In the game of Blackjack, the suits have no value and don't affect the hand whatsoever. The Ace of Hearts has the same value as the Ace of Spades, which is the same value as the other two Aces. (A rose, is a rose, is a rose). Aces count as either 1 or 11, whichever fits the hand best. That is the only card in which there is an option. The King, Queen, Jack, and Ten all count as 10 and are called 10's for simplicity. What's left is 2 through 9, which count as face value. The "pips" on the card correspond with their numerical value. Single and double deck games are "hand held" and dealt by the dealer from her hand. When four, six or eight decks are used, they are dealt from a rectangular box called a "shoe."

Don't fall asleep on me. We'll be into the real interesting "stuff" soon. Bear with me.

SHUFFLE, CUT AND BURN — Sounds like a law firm, doesn't it? Casinos don't want dealers spending a lot of time shuffling so they usually have guidlines that the dealer follows. As long as the cards are shuffled thoroughly 3 or 4 times, and also are "stripped" (the taking of small packets alternately from the top and bottom of the deck), the deck should be in a random order. Players are never allowed to shuffle the cards, no matter **who** they know.

Players **do** cut the cards and if all the players at the table refuse to cut, then the dealer performs this function.

A card is then burned, that is, discarded, by being placed in the discard rack. On shoe games, there are casinos that burn as many as 10 to 15 cards to discourage card counters.

When it's time to shuffle again, all the cards are placed face down on the table, and the whole process starts over.

THE BETTING — Before the deal begins, each player must place his bet in the betting square or circle. A player may play more than one hand, but the minimum bet increases if the player is going to have the privilege of doing this. Usually the rules are, twice the minimum for two hands and triple the minimum for three hands. When a player plays more than one hand he can only look at one hand at a time, and must complete the action (hit or stand) on that hand, before proceeding to the next.

He does not have a choice which hand he can look at first. It is always the hand closest to first base. I personally do not think you should play more than one hand unless you have reached the betting limit at the table, through an incredible winning streak, and want to bet more. Then you should "spread out" which means go to two hands.

THE DEAL — The dealer deals one card clockwise, from her left to right, and deals herself one card, and then deals the second card to each player in the same rotation and herself a card, to complete the deal. Many casinos deal all the players' cards face up from a shoe so there is no need for the players to handle the cards.

Decisions by the player are then made with a flick of the hand or finger in a "come on" motion when they want a hit, and a "halt" type motion, when they want to stay or stand. Dealing face up virtually eliminates almost everything a player can do to cheat the casino in a Blackjack game. I did say "almost," didn't I?

The dealer always has one card up and one card down. The down card is referred to as her "hole" card. The English style of Blackjack doesn't give the dealer a hole card. This eliminates the problem of the dealer exposing it, accidentally or otherwise. But it **creates** a problem by solving a problem. When the dealer has an ace or a ten up, and everyone acts on their hand, and some of the people who've acted on their hand make 21, and the dealer draws a ten or an ace respectively, she wins everyones money because she has a Blackjack. The players who have played out their hands and have gotten 21, all lose and boy, they get pissed. There are certain things the English do that just don't work in this country. That's one of them.

THE BLACKJACK — If the first two cards dealt to you were an Ace, and any King, Queen, Jack or Ten, you have a Blackjack. This is also referred to as a Natural or a Snapper. When you look at your hand and see an Ace and 10 count card, turn it over immediately and show it to the dealer. When she gets to your hand, she will pay you 1½ times your bet unless she also has a Blackjack. In that case you have a tie or "push." Everyone loses except anyone else with a Blackjack. They would also "push." When you "push" or tie, there is no action on the money you bet and, therefore, it is a standoff. Out of every thousand hands you should receive 44 Blackjacks, which works out to approximately one out of every 23 hands. Sometimes it seems like you get one every 23 months!

The dealer enjoys the same probabilty of receiving a Blackjack. Whenever her up-card is a 10 count card or an Ace, she checks her hole card to see if she has a Blackjack. If she has one, she turns her hole card over immediately and collects the bets. The only exception is if you have a Black

jack, which ties her, or if you take insurance. Insurance is a wager conceived by a genius who wanted the casinos to win more money. What you are actually doing when you take insurance, is betting the dealer has a Blackjack. Insurance can only be taken if the dealer has an Ace up. You place any amount up to ½ your bet, on the in-

Blackjack pays 1½ to 1, or 3 to 2.

surance line, and if she has the Blackjack, she takes your bet from the circle or square, and pays your insurance bet with that money. Some people think it's a "protection" bet, but if she doesn't have the Blackjack, you lose your insurance bet and you continue playing the hand. Now she has an Ace staring at you, and with an Ace as her up-card, she has a lot of room to make a hand that will beat you. Only card counters that are very proficient take insurance on rare circumstances. They do it only when the deck is "10 rich," that is, has lots of 10's left in it, in relation to the other cards left in the deck.

I recommend insurance **only** when you have a Blackjack. Percentage-wise insurance is **always** a bad bet. Why then, do I recommend it when you have a

Insuring a Blackjack.

Blackjack and the dealer has an Ace showing? Because this situation is not going to come up many times if you are a recreational player and play 5 or 6 times a year. When you do get a Blackjack I want to see you win something. If you are using my betting technique, and after 10 wins in a row get a blackjack, I don't want it tied. That situation may come up just once in your lifetime, and by God, I want you to win some money when it does. Let me climb off my soapbox so we can get on with this great game. I'm on a roll.

SIGNALLING, SPLITS AND DOUBLE DOWNS — No matter how noisy a casino is, the game of Blackjack can be played with relative ease, since everything can be accomplished through the use of signals. These signals are commonplace throughout the entire Gaming Industry, so once you learn them you can play anywhere. When you are first dealt your two cards face down, pick up the cards and total them, then look at the dealer's up-card and determine whether you will hit or stay.

If you want a hit (an additional card), wait until the dealer gets to you, since she starts with the player on first base, and then scrape the cards on the table **gently** in a motion towards your body. Continue this motion until you feel your hand is complete. The dealer will continue to give you additional cards face up until you stay or bust. If you stay, "tuck or slide" your cards under your money. If you bust or go over 21, turn your cards face up in front of your bet so the dealer can pick them up and collect your bet. You should decide whether you are going to hit or stay before the dealer gets to you. If your cards are tucked or slid under your money, she will go past you. When playing in a casino that deals all the players' cards face up, watch the other players before you sit down and you'll notice how they indicate to hit or stay. To hit, motion with your finger, gently scratching the table toward you, and to stay, wave your hand sideways, palm down. You can also use a "halt" motion, much the same as a traffic cop.

These motions are also used when you split a pair in a **face down** game. You look at your cards, determine you have a pair, and if you decide the best strategy is to split them, turn the pair face up. Spread the pair to indicate a split, and bet an additional amount equal to your bet, since you will actually be playing two independent hands. The signals used for these hands are the same used above in a game that is dealt face up. The only exception is a pair of Aces. You turn your Aces face up and match your bet, as if you're still playing two hands, but you only receive one card on each Ace, and this card is given face

22

down. You are allowed to look at these down cards but you cannot receive any additional hit cards no matter what the down cards are. If you happen to get two Aces as the down cards, on top of your two Aces, you cannot turn those Aces over and resplit them. Aces only call for one card face down on each, but it's still an excellent bet. **Always** split Aces when they are dealt to you.

To **double down** you turn both your cards face up, using caution not to spread them away from each other as you did in a split, and then match or equal your bet. When the dealer gets to your hand you will have your original bet in the circle or square with an equal stack right next to it, and both cards overlapped face up in front of the bets. She will give you one card face down and proceed to the next player. If you want to double down in a face up game, just match your original bet and tell the dealer you want to double down. Your double down card will also be dealt face up just as every other player's card is. This has absolutely no affect on you, since the dealer has no flexibility whatsoever on her hand. If she saw every player's hand and everyone had 12 and she had 16, she would still have to hit her hand.

YOUR HAND — The object of the game of Blackjack or 21, is for you to bring your card total to 21, or as near as possible to 21, without going over. If you go over 21 you "bust" and lose the hand immediately. One of the big advantages the casino enjoys is that you have to act before the dealer. If you go over 21 and "bust" with a 22, and the dealer plays out her hand and goes over 21, and "busts" with a 22, you have already lost your bet. Up until that point, if the dealer ties you, the bet is considered a push, which means you don't win or lose.

Once the cards are dealt by the dealer it is time to

make decisions that will affect the outcome of your wager. I designed the Blackjack Roadmap Chart in this book to give you consistent and correct decisions when you play. Practice at home and commit it to memory. If you haven't memorized it by the time you take your next trip, take it with you and look at it while you play.

Let's talk about the various hands you will encounter while playing. When you are first dealt your original two cards, if these two cards are any Ace and any 10 count card, you have a Blackjack and you turn your hand over and are paid 1½ times your bet (which is the same as 3 to 2). Any other two card combination is either called a "hard" hand or a "soft" hand. A "hard" hand is any hand whereby when you take a hit, you can bust. Hard hands are when your cards total 12 through 21. "Soft" hands are hands that include at least one Ace, and a hit will not break or bust the hand. You should become thoroughly familiar with "soft" hands since they come up about 10% of the time.

Examples of a hard hand are 10-2, 10-4, 9-7, 7-8, 4-3-9, 2-6-4, etc., etc. As you can see the next hit **could** bust the hand. "Soft" hand examples are A-2, A-5, A-8, 4-2-A, 3-5-A, 3-3-2-A. You can hit any of these hands and the hit will not bust or break the hand. The Ace is the only card with a dual value. It counts as 1 or 11 depending on what is most advantageous in that particular situation. The easiest method I know to handle a soft hand, is to count the first Ace as 11, and as soon as your total exceeds 21, count that Ace and any other you received as a hit, as 1. For example, if you were dealt an Ace and a 3 (A-3), you would have a soft 14 (Ace = 11 + 3 = 14).

Look at the Blackjack Roadmap and see what it tells

you to do with an A-3, if the dealers up-card is a 7. Did you look? What did it say? It says (H) which means hit. So you hit and receive a 9. Now you have a soft total of 23 which is over 21, so you count the Ace as 1 and you have a hard total of 13. Now what does the Roadmap say to do with a hard 13 against a dealer's 7? Find your hand of 13 and the corresponding square under the dealer's up-card of 7, and lo and behold, it says (H), which means hit again. Now you receive a 6 and you have a total of 19 and the Roadmap tells you to stand (ST). Deal out hands to yourself in your hotel room and you'll find how easy it Is to play a super game of Blackjack, with just a small amount of practice.

THE DEALER'S HAND — If you are the only player at the table and you bust, the dealer doesn't have to complete her hand. There's no sense to it if she does. If there are any active players left, the dealer will play out her hand. Remember, the dealer has no nerve racking decisions to make. Her actions are predetermined by the rules of the casino and most of those rules are standard throughout the Gaming Industry. If her count totals 17, 18, 19, 20, or 21, she must stay. If hor count is 16 or less she continues to hit her hand until the count reaches 17 or more, at which point she must stay. The only variation among casinos is when a dealer has a soft 17. In some, the rules require her to stay and in others, she is required to hit. Whatever the rule of the individual casino, it is usually printed across the layout above the insurance line. There is very little advantage or disadvantage from the player's standpoint, whether or not the dealer does or doesn't hit soft 17.

When the dealer has completed her hand, she starts with the first player on the right (3rd base), and moves around the table in a clockwise motion, making payoffs to players who have a higher count than hers. If you have the same count as the dealer it is a tie or a "push" and you don't win or lose your bet. If the dealer busts (goes over 21), she pays off each active player. All bets are paid off at "even money" except when a player receives a Blackjack. There are no "5 card Charlie's" as there are in a home game, and the player doesn't win the deal when he gets a Blackjack.

THIS PICTURE SHOWS HOW A BET FOR THE DEALER SHOULD BE PLACED.

TOKES OR TIPS — Dealers depend on tokes or tips as a big part of their salary. Here are some guidelines you may want to consider the next time you play. The dealer would rather have you bet for her instead of just giving her the money. This is fine but when would you bet for her? And where do you bet for her?

Money management is important throughout your trip and tipping is a part of money management. The easiest time to remember to bet for the dealer is when you get a Blackjack. If the dealer has been relatively nice to you and you feel comfortable, a tip is in order. A Blackjack should be dealt to you approximately once every 23 hands if you play for a relatively long period of time, and since you are paid 3 to 2 for a Blackjack, it affords the opportunity to bet for the dealer. The amount is up to you. If you get a Blackjack while betting $2, a $1 bet is appropriate for the dealer. If your bet was $10 you may want to bet $2 or $3 for her and if your bet was $100, you may want to bet $10 for her. Like I said, it's up to you.

Whatever the amount, the bet you make for the dealer is placed in front of your bet, barely outside the circle or square. She cannot parlay or let her bet ride. If she wins she must collect it, and if she loses, the bet goes into the rack just as your losing bet does.

SURRENDER — We will spend very little time on surrender since very few casinos offer it to you. It gives you the option to throw your hand away before you bust, as long as the dealer doesn't show an Ace as her up-card. For this privilege you forfeit half of your bet. Forget it.

BLACKJACK ROADMAP

I've named the following chart the "Blackjack Roadmap" because you use it exactly like a road-map. Look for your hand on the left, and follow the squares until you reach the dealer's up-card "square," and the symbol in the square tells you ex-actly what to do. Casinos don't mind if you have this in front of you, so tear it out of the book and use it whenever you play. In fact, a pit boss will probably converse with you to find out what it is, especially if you're winning. He'll probably want to buy one, and so will the dealer and the cocktail waitress. Get their addresses for me and I'll send them a price list. The strategy used in this chart makes the game of Blackjack an almost "even bet" for the player, if he follows it consistently. This strategy has been kept hermetically sealed in a mayonnaise jar on my grandmother's porch for many generations and I felt it was time to share it with the world.

Casino rules vary, therefore, in some squares there are two letters. If you are not allowed to do what the first letter says, then do what the second letter says. For example, if your hand was an A-7, and the dealer's up-card was a "6," it says D-ST. That means double down if the casino allows you to, and if they don't, then stand. When you "double down" you double your bet and turn both cards face up and the dealer gives you one down card. Some casinos do not afford this opportunity to you on any two cards, and have specific rules governing your double down options. To double down when the dealer has a vulnerable card showing, can mean increased pro-fits on your trip, and if done consistently, can make the difference between a winning trip, and a trip where you kick yourself in the ass all the way home.

The chart shows every combination of hands that can occur. Any time a 10 is referred to in Blackjack, it means a 10, or 10 count card, which include Kings, Queens, and Jacks as well as Tens. Familiarize yourself with the chart and deal yourself some hands at home, and you'll be playing the game of Blackjack as well as it can be played, which will hopefully be a satisfying and rewarding experience.

The Blackjack Roadmap was put on the following page, by itself, to make it easier to read and easier for you to tear out and keep next to your heart, where it belongs.

ST = STAND   H = HIT   Sp = SPLIT   D = DOUBLE DOWN
D-H = Double down if casino rules allow. Hit if they don't.
D-ST = Double down if casino rules allow. Stand, if they don't.

	YOUR HAND	DEALER'S UP-CARD 2	3	4	5	6	7	8	9	10	A
HARD HANDS	3 to 8	H	H	H	H	H	H	H	H	H	H
	9	D-H	D-H	D-H	D-H	D-H	H	H	H	H	H
	10	D	D	D	D	D	D	D	D	H	H
	11	D	D	D	D	D	D	D	D	D	D
	12	H	H	ST	ST	ST	H	H	H	H	H
	13	ST	ST	ST	ST	ST	H	H	H	H	H
	14	ST	ST	ST	ST	ST	H	H	H	H	H
	15	ST	ST	ST	ST	ST	H	H	H	H	H
	16	ST	ST	ST	ST	ST	H	H	H	H	H
	17	ST	ST	ST	ST	ST	ST	ST	ST	ST	ST
	18	ST	ST	ST	ST	ST	ST	ST	ST	ST	ST
	19	ST	ST	ST	ST	ST	ST	ST	ST	ST	ST
	20	ST	ST	ST	ST	ST	ST	ST	ST	ST	ST
	21	ST	ST	ST	ST	ST	ST	ST	ST	ST	ST
SOFT HANDS	A-2	H	H	D-H	D-H	D-H	H	H	H	H	H
	A-3	H	H	D-H	D-H	D-H	H	H	H	H	H
	A-4	H	H	D-H	D-H	D-H	H	H	H	H	H
	A-5	H	H	D-H	D-H	D-H	H	H	H	H	H
	A-6	D-H	D-H	D-H	D-H	D-H	H	H	H	H	H
	A-7	ST	D-ST	D-ST	D-ST	D-ST	ST	ST	H	H	ST
	A-8	ST	ST	ST	ST	ST	ST	ST	ST	ST	ST
	A-9	ST	ST	ST	ST	ST	ST	ST	ST	ST	ST
	A-10	ST	ST	ST	ST	ST	ST	ST	ST	ST	ST
PAIRS	A-A	Sp	Sp	Sp	Sp	Sp	Sp	Sp	Sp	Sp	Sp
	2-2	Sp	Sp	Sp	Sp	Sp	Sp	H	H	H	H
	3-3	Sp	Sp	Sp	Sp	Sp	Sp	H	H	H	H
	4-4	H	H	H	H	H	H	H	H	H	H
	5-5	D-H	D-H	D-H	D-H	D-H	D-H	D-H	D-H	H	H
	6-6	Sp	Sp	Sp	Sp	Sp	H	H	H	H	H
	7-7	Sp	Sp	Sp	Sp	Sp	Sp	H	H	H	H
	8-8	Sp	Sp	Sp	Sp	Sp	Sp	Sp	Sp	Sp	Sp
	9-9	Sp	Sp	Sp	Sp	Sp	ST	Sp	Sp	ST	ST
	10-10	ST	ST	ST	ST	ST	ST	ST	ST	ST	ST

CARD COUNTING

If you're not interested in card counting, skip this chapter. In any case, you **must** use the Blackjack Roadmap. If you don't plan on using either, all my hours of self denial in order to write this book, will have been in vain — and you'll never get past "go," and you'll never collect $200. (See Monopoly game for details.) Besides, it will really piss me off!

There are a handful of card counters that are actually a threat to the Gaming Industry. Can you be one of those threats? Probably not! It takes a hell of a lot of self discipline, and a good size bankroll. You also need the ability of being an actor, to not be branded a "card counter" by the casinos. Last, but not least, you need the determination of a kid from the ghetto, who wants to be a doctor. Did I paint too bleak a picture?

Card counting works — there is no question about it. To make it work as a profession you need all the ingredients I listed above. That would be at the highest level — the professional card counter; the guy who makes his living at it. But you don't want to make a living at card counting, you say! You're my kind of person. **Anyone** can learn how to count, and almost everyone uses a count even though they may not realize it. So much has been written about the subject of card counting that even the little old lady from a remote town in Kansas, knows that if she sees a lot of face cards and Aces come out when she is playing Blackjack, chances are, she won't get a Blackjack the next hand. So what does she do? She bets a smaller amount of money. This may be card counting in it's crudest form, but it's a form of card counting. I could bore you with many more examples that would just take up space, but I won't for now — unless you get on my nerves. There are still some people on this planet that don't believe card counting works. Believe me, it works.

Blackjack is one of the only casino games in which the house percentage varies with every card dealt. If just one card is removed from the deck, the deck percentage changes. However small this percentage is, it does change. Let me prove to you beyond a reasonable doubt (my attorney said that to the jury the last time my brother-in-law was on trial) that card counting is not only valid, but a force to be reckoned with. What if — 1) You and I were playing Blackjack and I was the dealer? 2) You were the greatest card counter in the Universe and had a photographic mind? 3) I dealt the cards down to the very end of the deck before I shuffled? 4) There were 6 cards left in the deck and I was about to deal them out? 5) These 6 cards were comprised of four 8's and two 7's? That's the "fantasy scenario." Now how much would you bet is there was no limit? The title to your car, the deed to your home and your bank account, would be a reasonable bet in this specific circumstance. The probability of you winning that hand is 100%. No matter what two card combination you receive you "stay." I, as the dealer, will either get a 7-7, or an 8-8 or an 8-7 and when I hit I'll "bust." I have to hit, the player doesn't. Therefore, when I take the hit card it will either be a 7 or an 8. This situation will probably never occur on this planet, and if it did, the player wouldn't be aware that it did. I just use it as an illustration that shows a deck can be 100% in the player's favor. There are extreme situations in the course of a Blackjack game, but usually none of this magnitude.

The basic principle of card counting is to bet more money when there are more Aces and 10 count cards left in the deck, and less money when there are less 10 count cards and Aces in the deck. Card counting makes you aware of these situations that occur during the normal course of the game so that you can vary your bet. You have the option of increasing the size of your bet when you know the deck is favorable, or decreasing your bet if it's unfavorable, and since you have this flexibility your chance of winning money at the end of a period of time are increased. Using the "Blackjack Roadmap" in this book makes the game an almost dead even bet for the player. This strategy, coupled with card counting, could make your gambling trips profitable and much more enjoyable.

I'm going to show you a real simple count that you should be able to learn in about 20 minutes, and if you practice, you should get pretty good in a few hours if you have average intelligence. **Everyone** has average intelligence. Everyone except my brother-in-law. Believe me, he's a real case. He'll make the medical journals someday. He claims he's the kid Babe Ruth visited in the hospital. When you look into his eyes you know nobody is driving. Anyway, where were we? Card counting, of course. Get a deck of cards and make sure all 52 cards are in the deck.

Take out an Ace, King, Queen, Jack and Ten and lay them face up on the table. These will be − 1 (minus one) count cards. So, on the table right now you have a total of − 5. Ace, King, Queen, Jack and Ten are a − 1 each, and that totals − 5.

CARDS WITH A " – 1" COUNT

Now take out a 7, 8, and 9 from the deck and put them on the table. These 3 cards are "zero" count cards. So now, when we total all 8 cards we have on the table, we still have – 5, since – 5 and zero = – 5. So far, how are we doing? Only one more step so bear with me.

CARDS WITH A ZERO COUNT

Take out a 2, 3, 4, 5 and 6 from the deck and lay them face up on the table. These 5 cards are + 1 count cards and total a + 5 if we add them together. **Now**, if we counted **all** the cards on the table, what would be our total? I hope you said zero because that's the answer. We have a −1, −1, −1, −1, −1, 0, 0, 0, +1, +1, +1, +1, +1. Add that all together and what have you got, bippidy, boppidy, boo. (Just a flashback of an old song. Excuse me.) Add that together and you have zero. We've now learned that you put a value of −1 on each Ace, King, Queen, Jack and Ten; a zero value on each 7, 8, and 9; and a +1 value on each 2, 3, 4, 5 and 6.

CARDS WITH A "+1" COUNT

Counting with speed is important in a Blackjack game, and in order to gain speed you'll have to do some practicing If you watch T.V., practice during the commercials. Just shuffle the deck and hold it in your hand face down and turn one card over at a time. The count is in the player's favor anytime it equals a plus. If it's a minus count, the casino has the advantage.

If you buy twenty dollars worth of chips from the dealer, your minimum bet will be $1 and your maximum bet will be dictated by the count. If the count is +4 you bet $4. If the count is +6 you bet $6. If the count is a minus or zero, your bet is $1.

Anytime the deck is minus or zero, you have no advantage so you bet the minimum. O.K. Let's shuffle up the deck and start practicing. We'll turn the cards over one at a time and go part way through the deck to get you started. The deck you shuffle is not going to be in the same order as the one I have, but this example should still help you.

CARD	CARD VALUE	INDIVIDUAL CARD COUNT	RUNNING TOTAL
1st	King	− 1	− 1
2nd	Queen	− 1	− 2
3rd	7	0	− 2
4th	8	0	− 2
5th	ACE	− 1	− 3

Right now we have seen 5 cards and they **total** a − 3 count. Let's continue. The deck is definitely not in our favor right now. Our bet would be the minimum allowed at the table.

CARD	CARD VALUE	INDIVIDUAL CARD COUNT	RUNNING TOTAL
6th	6	+ 1	− 2
7th	6	+ 1	− 1
8th	3	+ 1	0
9th	King	− 1	− 1
10th	Ace	− 1	− 2
11th	4	+ 1	− 1
12th	4	+ 1	0
13th	7	0	0

We're still at the minimum bet since the count is zero.

CARD	CARD VALUE	INDIVIDUAL CARD COUNT	RUNNING TOTAL
14th	8	0	0
15th	5	+ 1	+ 1
16th	4	+ 1	+ 2
17th	5	+ 1	+ 3
18th	7	0	+ 3
19th	King	− 1	+ 2
20th	3	+ 1	+ 3
21st	3	+ 1	+ 4
22nd	2	+ 1	+ 5

We now have a deck that has turned in your favor. A + 5 running total count means a bet of $5 if you were playing, and had this type of count. The bigger the plus (+) count, the more percentage is in your favor to win your next hand. This method of play is good because it **controls** your betting patterns. Instead of having your emotions controlling your bets, you are playing like the professionals and the cards are dictating the amount you will bet. Whenever the dealer shuffles, you go to the minimum bet, since the deck is starting at a zero count. This count can be applied to any Blackjack game, with any amount of decks.

When you walk up to a game, just play the minimum bet allowed until the shuffle. You have to start counting **after** the shuffle. Some casinos burn or bury 15 to 20 cards to slow card counters down. That's all it does. It slows them down, but doesn't stop them from counting. Start at zero no matter how many cards they burn or bury. There are many sophisticated card counting techniques that you may want to investigate, but this type of book is for beginners and the count I've shown you is effective and simple.

Once you feel comfortable that you've mastered going through a complete deck of cards and can keep track of the count turning over one card at a time, you should advance to the next step, which is turning "**two**" cards over at a time. This is not difficult since you're already familiar with the point count of each of the various cards, and in a short time you'll be able to get through the complete deck in less than 1 minute. I do it in 32 seconds, and I'm no rocket scientist.

Whether you go through the deck practicing with one card being turned over, or two cards being turned over, there is a very simple way to check your accuracy. The deck starts at a zero count and after all 52 cards are turned over, should end up a zero count. If you wind up with any number but zero, you've miscounted and should turn the deck over and start again. Accuracy is important, so take your time and try to build up speed as time goes on. Learning this chapter may take awhile, as most people don't have the time required to learn a Blackjack count system. I can understand that. I'm a very understanding person. But, don't ever, ever, ever, play Blackjack again without using the strategy mapped out in the "Blackjack Roadmap." I cannot say this to you too many times.

If you decide that you want to try and use this count strategy, then play third base. This allows you to see more cards and could possibly help your play.

MONEY MANAGEMENT TECHNIQUE

If you use only the "Blackjack Roadmap" and nothing else, you will have an excellent playing technique based on millions of years of computer technology (sometimes I tend to exaggerate), but you will have no betting control. This worries me. Card counting gives you your unit bet, along with a knowledgeable and sound pattern of play, by using the Blackjack Roadmap in conjunction with the count. The bets that the count system dictates can be any denomination. A + 3 count is just telling you to bet 3 units. If you play dollars, then it would mean $3. If you play $5 chips then it would mean 3 units of $5 each, or $15. Your minimum bet would be $5 on a zero or minus count, as it would be $1 if you were a $1 chip player. If you only use the Blackjack Roadmap, and no count system, you **need** a betting technique.

This betting technique was designed just for you. The columns are set up to show you what to do if you win or lose each hand. You start with a 1 unit bet. If you're a big bettor and you normally play $5, $25, or $100 chips, then apply the unit number in column one, to your size chip. You can use this technique with any size bankroll. Let's assume you buy-in $100 and you receive 20 five dollar chips or checks, as they are known in the Gaming Industry. Your first bet would be 1 unit or 1 five dollar check. If you win the bet, you add 1 five dollar check to your bet, totalling 3 units. (The one you added, the one you bet originally, and the one you won. A total of 3.) If you lose the 3 unit bet you revert back to 1 unit. The chart should now be easy to follow. Tear it gently from this book and keep it with you on your next trip. If you don't use the count system, this chart will help you Immensely in determining how much to bet. In any case, USE THE BLACKJACK ROADMAP. (There I said it again and I'm glad.)

IF YOUR LAST BET

	WAS	AND YOU	YOU NOW BET
a)	1	LOST	1
b)	1	WON	3
c)	3	LOST	1
d)	3	WON	3 AGAIN
e)	3 AGAIN	LOST	1
f)	3 AGAIN	WON	6
g)	6	LOST	1
h)	6	WON	6 AGAIN
i)	6 AGAIN	LOST	1
j)	6 AGAIN	WON	12
k)	12	LOST	1
l)	12	WON	12 AGAIN
m)	12 AGAIN	LOST	6 GO BACK TO LINE (g) OR (h) AFTER THIS BET
n)	12 AGAIN	WON	15
o)	15	LOST	6 GO BACK TO LINE (g) OR (h) AFTER THIS BET
p)	15	WON	15 AGAIN
q)	15 AGAIN	LOST	6 GO BACK TO LINE (g) OR (h) AFTER THIS BET
r)	15 AGAIN	WON	20
s)	20	LOST	6 GO BACK TO LINE (g) OR (h) AFTER THIS BET
t)	20	WON	20 AGAIN
u)	20 AGAIN	LOST	6 GO BACK TO LINE (g) OR (h) AFTER THIS BET

If you get to this point and run out of chart, it means you have won 11 in a row and you are a 90 unit winner, not counting the Blackjack, double down, and split money, you've won along the way. Not bad for a 20 unit buy-in. The "streak" may not be over and there's no telling how many hands you may win in a row so if you get to this point and run out of chart, double your bet every other time when you win. For example, if you win the 25 unit bet, bet 25 units again, then 50 units, then 50 units again, then 100 units, then 100 units again, etc., etc., until you reach the casino limit. Then spread out to two hands at the limit, and then 3 hands at the table limit. Do this AS LONG AS YOUR STREAK CONTINUES, AND YOU KEEP WINNING. As soon as you lose a hand, revert back to your 6 unit bet and lines (g) or (h) depending on the outcome of the 6 unit wager. Use your Blackjack Roadmap religiously while playing this money management technique, and if it requires you to double down or split, with a large bet at stake, do it. Don't let the size of your bet vary your play.

When you play Blackjack for a period of time, you will enjoy long winning streaks as well as losing streaks. You may not **enjoy** losing streaks but they're a sad reality of the game. This betting technique assures you of minimum bankroll losses, even if you happen to lose 20 hands in a row. If you do lose 20 hands in a row, and believe me you will, if you play enough Blackjack, don't call me and tell me some sad story, that you started betting more after you lost the 10th hand, because you didn't think you could possibly lose another one. And by the time you lost the 20th hand, you blew the family farm and the worst part is yet to come — you have to tell the family. If you follow my chart, that can never happen. If it does, it's your own fault so don't tell me about it. I don't want to hear it.

SYSTEMS IN GENERAL

Systems in general "suck." That may be a graphic word but sometimes I have to get graphic to get your attention and keep it. Most systems have you betting larger amounts of money as you lose, so that you can recoup your losses with one big bet. This logic is totally illogical and borders on being immoral, impractical and really and truly sucks. The only salvation you have with any betting system, is that it offers a means of controlling your money **if** and only **if** it allows you to bet more when you WIN, not LOSE, and limits your losses when you do lose. If someone tells you they have an infallible system, ask them six months later how it's doing. Chances are they'll be borrowing money from you before that time. If it sounds too good to be true — it is.

IN CONCLUSION

If this book helps out just one person, I can go to bed tonight a happy man. If you study it and follow it, you might go to bed happy too. There are no sure bets in anything, but there are definitely good and bad methods of play. What you've read is a collection of over 20 years of knowledge in the gaming business. You're much better off listening to someone with that much experience than you are listening to your brother-in-law talk about his infallible system. I learned a long time ago not to listen to mine. Anyone who is 6'2" and weighs 310 lbs., whose hobby is ice-dancing, and who looks good in a beanie, I have reservations about.

I hope you enjoyed this book and use the valuable information on your next gambling journey. If you do, you'll surely be "Playing to Win." See you around...

P.S. Read the Glossary. It's humorous and informative.

BLACKJACK GLOSSARY

What you always wanted to know but were afraid to ask. The following definitions are all true at some point in time.

ACE — a) A card in Blackjack that can be counted as a 1 or 11. b) The highest card in the deck. c) A character in most Air Force movies.

BASIC STRATEGY — a) Method of play used by knowledgeable players. b) An excellent strategy for Blackjack. c) The plan you formulate in your car or the plane on the way to your favorite casino. d) The plan you formulate on the way home from your favorite casino, which you plan to use the next time you visit your favorite casino.

BET — a) A friendly wager between two parties on an event that is supposed to occur at some point in time. b) What every casino owner wants you to do before you unpack your luggage.

BET THE LIMIT — To bet as much as the casino will allow you, either to win more money or impress the people with you.

BLACKJACK — a) Any Ace, with a K, Q, J or 10. These two cards should be turned over and shown to the dealer as soon as you discover you have a Blackjack. b) A seldom seen weapon also known as a "sap." c) What my son learned to play when he was four.

BREAK — a) Cards totalling over 21. b) What used to happen in the "old days" to someone's hand if they were caught cheating.

BREAK-IN DEALER — Common terminology throughout the Gaming Industry for a beginning dealer. The break-in period usually lasts for 6 months to a year, but I've seen dealers who have been in the business for 5 years, that are still in the break-in category. Their minds seem to hover around the planet Jupiter most of the time.

BREAKING HAND — a) A hard 12, 13, 14, 15, or 16.

These are considered breaking hands and will break with a one card draw. b) In the "old days" when Bruno the bouncer grabbed you, and you asked him what he was doing, this would be his reply.

BURN A CARD — To remove a card from play. This is usually done with the top card of every new shuffle. In some casinos as many as 20 or 30 cards may be burned, especially on 4 and 6 deck shoes.

BUST — a) Cards totalling over 21. b) What you notice when you see a showgirl.

BUY-IN — An exchange between you and the dealer whereby you give the dealer currency for casino checks or chips.

CALL BET — a) A verbal bet made by the player as he is getting his money out of his pocket. This bet is not always accepted by casinos. b) Call bets are never accepted by Call Girls.

CARD COUNTING — A strategy used by sophisticated players. The basic element in card counting is to bet more money when the deck percentage is in your favor. The deck constantly changes with each card that is dealt, so there is credibility to this method of play.

CASING A DECK — Counting cards and watching each card with intensity.

CASINO — a) A place to have fun where games of chance are conducted for your enjoyment. b) The place you hope pays off your mortgage and allows you to retire with an initial "investment" of $300. c) The place where you can't wait to get to, and eight hours later, can't wait to get away from.

CASINO MANAGER — a) The person in charge of the casino operation. b) The person whose name you hear constantly paged. c) The person who has the agonizing task of picking the people to be laid off at Christmas time. d) Mr. Nice Guy.

CHECKS — a) Terminology used for "chips" which are used at all casino games in place of currency. Each check usually costs the casino about 30¢ so they encourage them to be taken home as souvenirs. $5 checks are usually red, $25 checks are usually green, and $100 checks are usually black. Casinos use an assortment of colors that are "inlaid" around the outer edge of their checks, and these "inlays" are unique to each casino operation. Manufacturers of these checks are licensed by the State and very tight controls are used to ensure against duplication. b) A piece of paper you sign to receive currency, so that you can play for a longer period of time, with money you were going to use for something else.

CHIPS — a) Frequently used term on a Roulette Wheel to identify "Wheel Chips" as opposed to "Casino Checks." Wheel Chips are various colors that have no set value, whereas casino checks have a definite value stamped in the center of them. b) A food used at parties and while watching T.V. that tastes especially good with a dip.

CREDIT MANAGER — a) A casino executive who decides how much credit the casino will extend to you. b) The person who bought your gold watch the last time you played and went broke. c) The tall guy with the short neck who okays your checks.

CUT — a) The division of the deck by a player after the dealer shuffles. b) To say something derogatory about someone. c) What your kid comes home with, after he falls down while playing. d) To skip a class in high school.

DEAL — a) The distribution of cards to players by the dealer. b) What your brother-in-law came to you with, and you lost your shirt.

DEALER — a) The person on the table you give your money to, in exchange for casino chips. b) The friendly person you look forward to seeing and tipping each time you visit your favorite casino. c) The person who told you the next time you bent a card he was going to take your margarita and pour it in your ear.

DOUBLE DOWN — To double the size of your bet and receive only one additional card.

DRAW — a) To receive additional cards. This feat is accomplished by lightly scraping your original two cards along the table toward your body. b) To take your gun out of a holster when you're in a duel.

DROP BOX — a) Also called "cans." b) The box located under the table that stores all your hard earned money until the next morning, when it's counted. The drop boxes are changed every shift and are kept in the "soft count room." Paper money is referred to as "soft" while coins from the slot machines are called "hard."

EYE IN THE SKY — a) Terminology used for the person who is out of sight watching surveillance cameras, or observing you and the dealer through one way mirrors. The dealer watches the players, the floormen and pit bosses watch the dealers **and** the players, the shift boss watches the floormen and pit bosses, the casino manager watches the shift boss, the owner watches the casino manager, the eye in the sky watches everyone, and I believe some casinos have a helicopter hovering overhead, watching the eye in the sky. b) GOD.

FACE CARD — Any King, Queen or Jack. If you don't know what a face card is, you have led a very sheltered life.

FIRST BASE — a) First position at a Blackjack table. This person receives the first hand dealt by the dealer. b) What you try and reach on your first encounter with a beautiful woman.

FLOORMAN — a) A supervisor of the gaming tables. b) Another term for pit boss or pit supervisor. The chain of command in a casino is dealer, boxman, floorman, pit boss, shift boss and casino manager. c) A term used for slot supervisors. d) A term used for department store supervisors.

FUN BOOK — a) A casino promotional item that usually includes many free items. b) The book you are reading.

GET OUT — a) To be a loser and get even. b) What your wife yells at you when you come home a loser.

HIT — a) A term used by players to draw additional cards. These cards are numerically added to your original two cards. b) What bad guys do to people they don't like.

HOLE CARD — a) The dealer's down card. b) The plan you've devised if everything you planned goes wrong.

HOOKER — a) A lady of the night. b) The reason your wife doesn't allow you to go on gambling trips alone.

HOUSE ADVANTAGE — a) The percentage in favor of the house. b) When you are causing a disturbance and nine casino security guards approach you.

INSURANCE — A bet you are allowed to make when the dealer has an Ace showing. You may bet any amount up to one half of your original bet. Insurance pays 2 to 1 and in actuality, you are betting that the dealer has a Blackjack. If she does have one, you have protected your original bet. If she doesn't have one, then she takes your insurance money and you proceed with the hand.

LAYOUT — a) The cloth used on the gaming tables. Layouts cost $55 for Blackjack, $250 for Craps and $200 for Roulette. b) What customers spill drinks on, and burn holes in, almost immediately after they are changed.

LIMIT — a) The maximum amount that can be bet. b) What people tell their friends they bet when they get home.

MARKER — a) An I.O.U. that you sign. b) A piece of paper you wish you didn't sign when you get home. c) The last name of a kid I went to high school with.

MONEY MANAGEMENT — a) One of the most important aspects of playing any game. It is the control of your money during the course of the game. b) What your wife tries to accomplish with your paycheck each week.

NATURAL — a) A Blackjack. b) The name of a movie starring Robert Redford. c) What health food stores publicize.

PARLAY — a) To stack up your winning bet and bet the whole thing again. b) What you do when you're losing and trying to get even.

PAT — a) A hand that the player decides to stay on, refusing any additional cards. b) What you do to your back when you go home a winner.

PERCENTAGE — What the casino operates on. This number varies on different bets and different games.

PIT — a) The area located behind the Blackjack or Craps tables. Only casino personnel are allowed in this area. b) The place you almost walked into, the last time you were in a casino. You knew you were in a sensitive area, when that nice pit boss grabbed you by the throat and escorted you out.

PIT BOSS — a) A gaming supervisor who is responsible for a specific gaming area. This person is either a man or a woman and usually smokes thick expensive cigars. Men are more apt to smoke the thick ones and women the expensive ones. b) A person that is paid to watch gaming activities and is programmed to look extremely concerned at all times. c) A coffee cup on the pit stand.

PIT STAND — a) An edifice in the pit made from Imported wood, that includes a telephone, drawers where new cards and dice are kept, and sometimes a bookkeeper who keeps track of credit play. b) A large wooden structure in the pit area that can usually hold up to 17 coffee cups. c) A place to congregate in the pit area and tell stories and jokes. These jokes **always** bring a response of laughter if told by an owner of the casino or the Casino Manager. No casino owner or Casino Manager has ever told an unfunny joke to any employee.

TERMINATE — a) A nice word for "fired." b) The consequences when you think a joke is unfunny. c) "(b)" is an exaggeration. d) Sometimes it takes two unfunny jokes.

PUSH — To tie the dealer. If you both have the same hand it is considered a tie or push and there is no action on the hand.

SHIFT BOSS — a) Also called Shift Manager. A casino executive who has usually worked himself up through the ranks. He is in charge of the complete shift of casino employees, and in smaller operations is responsible for the entire property when the Casino Manager is not there. b) The person waiting for the Casino Manager to get fired or die, because he knows he can do a better job.

SHILL — A games starter hired by the casino to entice you to play a game. Most customers feel uneasy about being the first one to play at a dead game, and shills are used to not give you that feeling. There is nothing wrong with playing with a shill at the game. Many shills are older people and it gives them a chance to be employed and provide an important function.

SHOE — a) A dealing device used to hold two or more decks of cards. b) What I have trouble buying, since I wear a 15EEE.

SHUFFLE — a) To rearrange the cards before dealing. This act is done by the dealer in a very professional manner so as not to expose any cards. b) A dance step popular in the 30's.

SOFT HAND — a) A hand in which you cannot break. A soft hand always includes an ace. b) What your wife used to have before she started doing the dishes for you 25 years ago.

SPLITTING — To divide a pair of numerically identical cards and develop each as a separate hand.

STAND — a) To refuse any additional cards and stay with the cards you have. b) What you do when you hear the Star Spangled Banner.

STIFF — a) Any breaking hand with a two card total

of 12, 13, 14, 15, or 16. b) How you feel when you wake up the next day after playing 17 hours straight.

SYSTEM — An aggravating method of play in which you will lose your money and not have any fun in the process.

TEN-RICH — Card counters terminology which means there is an abundance of 10 count cards remaining in the deck, in relation to the other cards which remain.

THIRD BASE — a) Last position at the Blackjack table. This person receives the last hand dealt by the dealer. b) The place that people stare at when you make the wrong decision, and the dealer "makes" her hand.

TOKE — a) A tip. b) What every dealer looks for when you win. c) A gratuity.

UP-CARD — The dealer's face-up card.

86'd — A term used when someone is thrown out (sometimes literally) of a casino. He is usually read the "trespass act" by a security guard and the welcome mat is pulled from under his feet. He is never again invited to the Christmas party and usually has his fun book taken away.

ANSWERS - ANSWERS - ANSWERS

As you may have guessed the answers are the same regardless of the bet. Consistency is an important part of gambling. For some reason when people bet **more**, it alters their style of play. Casinos enjoy huge profits each year because of inconsistent uneducated play. Don't let the size of your bet dictate your play. O.K., here are the answers I know you've been anxiously waiting for.

1) Always hit a 6 and Ace (soft seventeen). If the dealer has a 2, 3, 4, 5 or 6 showing, double down. Casinos hit a soft seventeen, so it must be the right thing to do. Besides that, my Apple Computer says it's the right thing to do.

2) Always split Aces. Whenever you play 21 don't overplay your bankroll. In other words, never make a bet so big that you can't double down or split cards if the occasion arises. If you only have $20 to play and you bet $10 or $15 on one hand, and a double down or split situation occurs, you won't be able to take advantage of it. Unless, of course, you use the money you said you wouldn't use, no matter what.

3) It should excite you. At my age there aren't too many things that excite me, but seeing all the 5's fall is exciting. The five is **the** most important card in the deck for the dealer. That's right. **The** most important. "Why," you ask? Since the dealer **has** to hit any hand up to 16, the 5 is a critical card for them. If the dealer has 12 the 5 makes a 17, if they have 13, a 5 makes them an 18, etc. The less 5's in the deck, the more of a chance they have of "breaking" or going over 21. If the dealer doesn't shuffle on you, then increase the size of your bet. I usually double my

bet if I see all the 5's are out. Hugging the dealer is forbidden under Nevada law. Besides that, your wife or husband may not understand. Besides that, the pit boss may not understand.

4) The single deck offers the best advantage to you. If you can afford the minimum bet then by all means play the single deck. In Tahoe and Reno, single decks are common and you can still bet $1 or $2 a hand. Atlantic City uses 4 and 6 deck shoes and the cards are all dealt face up. There isn't much choice in that situation so if you want to play 21, you have to play the shoe. Under those conditions read and study the section on card counting, as it will be invaluable to you. If it's not, I've heard this book brings about 35¢ at swap meets.

5) Absolutely. Against a 6 you should do whatever you can as the dealer is at a distinct disadvantage. This does **not** include splitting face cards. You have an **almost** sure winner with two face cards. Besides that, people at the table will stare at you and spill their drink in your lap, and probably say obscene things about your heritage, especially if they lose because of your decision to split face cards or tens.

6) Again, you have the opportunity to double your bet when the dealer has a 6 showing so "go get 'em." Double down on 10 every time **except** when the dealer shows a face card, 10, or an Ace. Double down on 11 **every** time no matter what the dealer has showing.

7) If you ever split 10's or face cards, I'll never talk to you again.

8) Hit the 12. I hit 12 anytime the dealer has a 7

showing and I keep hitting until I get at least 17. So, if you have a 12 and the dealer has a 10 showing, hit it, until you get at least 17.

9) Insurance is a controversial subject with me. My own personal opinion is to take insurance only when **you** have a Blackjack (any 10 or face card and Ace). If you have a $10 bet and the dealer has an Ace up and you have a Blackjack, you will win $10 by insuring your bet, whether or not the dealer has the Blackjack. You are ensured of winning whatever your wager is. If you don't insure your bet and the dealer turns over a Blackjack, it's a tie, and you don't win or lose anything. I would rather see you win the $10 for sure.

Insurance costs you ½ of your bet and in actuality, you're betting the dealer has a Blackjack. Professional players who play every day have shown me computer printouts which show a small percentage against the player who takes insurance. First of all, I do not advocate insurance all the time. Just when you have a Blackjack. Also, since you are a recreational player who plays periodically, the situations you will encounter to have the percentages work against you may take a lifetime. I would rather see you win the $10 now. You could walk from San Francisco to Las Vegas and not find $10 on the side of the road. Of course, it depends on what side of the road you walk on.

10) Even if you hate the guy in the office it would be difficult to double down on 12. Besides that, if you did and caught a 9 (God forbid) you might get hooked on doubling down on 12. **Never** double on any 2 cards that constitute a breaking hand (10-2, 10-3, 10-4, 10-5, 10-6, etc.). There are

situations when you should double down on an ace and a 2, 3, 4, 5, 6 or 7. But in these circumstances you cannot break. These are called "soft hands" and when the dealer has a 5 or 6 showing it could be very advantageous for you to double with a "soft hand."

11) Weren't we just talking about that? Amazing perception. When the dealer has a 5 or 6 up, he or she is very vulnerable. These are the times that will determine whether or not you'll be a winner or loser for the trip. You have to take advantage of these situations. That's why it's important not to make a bet so big that you can't double down or split. They are not guaranteed situations and you won't win every time, but you have a distinct advantage and must capitalize on these situations.

12) Stay on 12 if the dealer has a 4, 5 or 6 showing.

13) The winner is behind door (b). Double down on 10 anytime the dealer has any card showing but a face card, 10 or an Ace. Never split 5's unless you're on a self destruction trip and you want to give all your money away before your kids inherit it. If that's the case, call me and I'll deal to you in the privacy of your home.

14) I like (c) — spill your drink and really get the dealer pissed, especially if you're drinking tomato juice. Dealing is a gruelling job. Dealers usually work 1 hour on and 20 minutes off. They stand in one spot, their backs ache, their feet swell, and many of them sweat. This does not condone rudeness. Attitude is an important part of their job and many of them take pride in their work and are friendly most of the time. Find a

dealer you are comfortable with. There's a lot of them in every casino that will fit your criteria.

15) Never hit a "hard" 17 (face card and a 7) unless you saw the dealer's hole card and you know she has you beat.

16) If you drink, it's difficult not to drink excessively when it's free. It's free because it's the casino's secret weapon. The more you drink the more your judgement will be altered. Have a few drinks if you must, while you play, but save the serious drinking for the bar. And then use the local taxi service to get to your motel. My kids might be outside playing.

17) Dealers make $50,000 to $75,000 a year only if they're stealing. Casinos pay their dealers between $28 and $35 a shift (8 hours). "Tips" or "tokes" as they are called in the industry are an important part of their livelihood. Tahoe casinos average $30 - $60 a day, downtown Vegas $20 - $40 a day, Las Vegas Strip $50 -$100 a day, and Atlantic City $50 - $80 a day. These "tokes" are taxable income and many dealers wind up with paychecks of $1. That's right. One Dollar. The tips are added to their paycheck and tax is taken out on that amount, and then the tips are subtracted. Most casinos let their dealers split their tips daily and they receive the cash daily. The average dealer makes far less than $20,000 a year. Usually the husband and wife both work, and on different shifts, so one of them can be home to take care of the kids. No wonder the divorce rate is so high.

18) Absolutely. A pit boss is a valuable ally. If you

are a decent player you are a valued customer. All customers are valued customers but there are different attitudes in the numerous casinos regarding players. In some casinos a player who plays between $5 and $25 a hand for his stay, is entitled to comp privileges. In other casinos, they don't even look at you. Don't be afraid or embarrassed to ask for a comp dinner or even a comp room. You might be pleasantly surprised! This just gives you more gambling money for your trip.

) Stop at the casino cashier. Never take large amounts of money to your room because it is simply not safe. All casinos have a method in which you can deposit the money in their cage, and it only takes 30 seconds to fill out the form. If you are out on the town and find you need more money, most casinos will arrange for you to get the money you have deposited at another casino, if you are playing at their casino. If a casino knows they can win $2,000 or more from you, they will do everything possible to make it convenient for you to retrieve your money. That's why so many casinos have Visa and Master Charge phones near their casino cages. What a bonanza that has turned out to be. They're hoping someday you can get cash on your Sears or library card.

) I'm working on the needlepoint book.

) It is my sincere wish that this book helps you in attaining more winning sessions than you normally experience. That is enough satisfaction for me. Along with the money you paid for this.

DID YOU ENJOY THIS BOOK?

Other books available in the "Playing to Win" Series by Tony Korfman include Baccarat, Craps, Keno, Poker, Roulette, and Slots. Published and Distributed by Gaming Books International, Inc. 1512 E. Fremont St. Las Vegas, Nevada 89101. Send $3 for each book, or include your Visa or MasterCard number. Don't forget to include the expiration date. We pay all postage, handling, freight, tax, license, insurance, transportation and delivery, to or near your home. Such a deal!!!

FOR MORE INFORMATION ON GAMBLING.

Gambler's Book Club, world's largest gambling bookstore, will send you upon request, a free 28-page catalog listing more than 1,000 in-print titles. The catalog is updated annually and has more than a dozen sections that include all phases of gambling.

The store is owned by John and Edna Luckman and their motto is "Knowledge is Protection." For your free catalog drop a note to Gambler's Book Club, 630 South 11th Street, Las Vegas, Nevada 89101 or call the store, toll free at 1-800-634-6243. The store is very reputable and I buy all my books there. Would you believe I buy **some** of my books there? This is NOT a paid political announcement.

Tony Korfman
Author

GAMING BOOKS INTERNATIONAL
MAIL ORDER DISCOUNTS
ORDER 5 BOOKS GET THE 6TH ONE FREE!
FOR CREDIT CARD ORDERS OR C.O.D. PLEASE CONTACT GAMING BOOKS INTERNATIONAL, 1512 E. FREMONT, LAS VEGAS, NV 89101, (702) 477-7771

1. GIANT LAS VEGAS FUN PAK . . .

This little goody has over $300 in coupon values. It covers almost all of the big places on the Strip and downtown as well. Each pak contains lots and lots of coupons worth all kinds of freebies in every place you use them . . . a BIG PAK . . . for a small price, just $6.

2. SUCCESSFUL SLOT SYSTEMS . . .

Are you tired of aching shoulders and sore elbows? Does your back start to tighten up after hours of sitting only to find out that you are playing the wrong machine? Put an end to all of this misery by reading this helpful guide. It is a book of the most successful slot systems. Some of these systems were found by the author on his trip to Vegas. Others were uncovered by coaxing successful slot players to reveal their systems for winning. Some of the very systems in this book are being sold separately today for as much as $20. This is a real bargain for a serious slot player. We sell this book for only $6.

3. HOT SLOTS . . .

In over 20 trips, the author claims to have at least paid his expenses via the slots. Read such topics as: Why I Can't Lose, Budgets and Systems for Winning, How to Find a HOT SLOT!, and the list goes on. The best "inside" subject of slot playing for profit. Just $6.

4. LUCKY SLOTS! How to Beat the Casino Bandits . . .

Which machines to play, which casinos to haunt, and how to leave while darker side how casino slots are set; how odds are calculated, and the real truth and possible locations of "loose" machines. Includes several winning systems. Only $6.

5. SUCCESSFUL CASINO SYSTEMS . . .

This book covers winning systems broken down into three sections; BLACKJACK, ROULETTE, and CRAPS. Each section gives information on money management and other important subjects that are helpful to you. It's like getting THREE BOOKS IN ONE! Made to retail at up to $10. It's yours for just $6.

6. SUCCESSFUL KENO SYSTEMS . . .

In almost every Las Vegas casino, the fascinating game of Keno can award prizes of $50,000. It is not hard to play but it is best to know the RIGHT WAY. This unusual book reveals systems on number selection for single and multiple tickets. It is a must if you are going to play Keno. $6.

7. SECRETS OF WINNING AT CASINO ROULETTE . . .

Learn the grand game of roulette from ground zero to grand expertise! Sophisticated and little-known techniques such as clocking the wheel (or dealer), action numbers and multi-number payoffs. How to set win goals and loss limits. While no system is foolproof, this book offers several based on countless thousands of winning bets. $6.

8. SECRETS OF ATTRACTING GOOD LUCK . . .

This amazing book written by Dr. Vincent A. Grantz will explain to you what good and bad luck really is, how to "cause" yourself to be lucky, all about gambling and good luck, and many more mezmerizing and interesting subjects. This book sells for just $6 a copy.

9. ANYONE CAN WIN MONEY AT GREYHOUND RACING . . .

This book guides you step-by-step in the basic rules of handicapping and offers tips on how to wager, money management, how to spot potential winners, and much more. Even the most experienced will find help in acquiring additional unique handicapping techniques and methods. By reading this book you and your wallet will soon find out that greyhound racing has become your most profitable and enjoyable sport! $6.

10. SUCCESSFUL HORSE RACING . . .

Here's a book that's all about the fine art of betting intelligently. It will make money for you from day one! All of your questions will be answered when you are finished reading this book. So take the "gamble" out of selections and beat the races today! $6.

11. THE ART OF BETTING HORSES AND WINNING CONSISTENTLY . . .

By reading this book you will come away not only with a solid groundwork of the sport but a unique skill to pick and choose the best horses in any given race. Only $6.

12. HOW TO MAKE MONEY AT THE HARNESS RACES . . .

This book supplies information about what harness racing is all about. What the program will look like when it's a chart. The horse to bet and what to stake. Only $5.95.

13. MAKING MONEY WITH RACEHORSE BETTING SYSTEMS . .

Find out how to stake. How much you need plus two systems for the daily double and three systems for forecast bets. Only $9.50.

4. PICKING WINNERS AT THE HARNESS RACES . . .

Principles and techniques of harness handicapping; How to analyze past performances correctly; Understand grades and class differences, consistency, longshots. How to bet and win trifectas, quinelas, exactas and doubles. $6.

5. WINNING CONSISTENTLY AT THE GREYHOUND RACES . . .

This book shows how you can pick a much higher percentage of winning dogs. Examines betting and money systems, handicapping, chart interpretation, and rating systems. How to win exotic bets: Trifectas, quinelas, exactas and doubles. Includes simplified systems you can depend on year after year. $6.

6. HOW I WON 2,000 SWEEPSTAKES PRIZE CONTESTS . . .

This book will reveal some new tricks on how to win. It will show you how to win top money in the old contest favorites such as; "finish this sentence in twenty-five words or less," and the ever popular "name the product". Read this book carefully and you may find that it will pay sizable dividends to you and your family. Good luck! $6.

7. JOKE BOOK . . .

One of the last American made souvenirs. This book is written by Jimmy K who is known for his local humor. This humorous book will have you rolling on the floor. For such a small price you will get a lot of laughs. $4.00.

8. HOW TO WIN AT BLACKJACK, "WITHOUT COUNTING CARDS" . . .

Are you tired of Counting Cards? Are you tired of Playing "22"? Finally a No Card Counting System For Winning at BLACKJACK! COUNT MONEY NOT CARDS! A UNIQUE, NEW COPYRIGHTED Combination of MONEY MANAGEMENT and a PROVEN Uncomplicated System. Only $9.95.

9. ADVANCE BLACKJACK SYSTEM . . .

A must for the professional blackjack player. Wins 9 out Of 10 times. Expensive but worth it. Advance Blackjack Strategy included. $100.00.

0. ADVANCE BLACKJACK STRATEGY . . .

An improved strategy to help you win every time. A must for you blackjack pros. Only $10.00.

1. BLACKJACK SYSTEM, LIVE BLACKJACK HANDS . . .

Try your blackjack system from live blackjack hands played in Las Vegas. Over 2500 live blackjack hands played in casinos on the strip and downtown. Results of wins, losses, doubles, splits, and blackjack. Try your system on these recorded blackjack hands and be ready to beat the tables. Only $6.00.

22. HOW TO WIN AT VIDEO POKER . . .

This book beats the poker machines with ruthless efficiency when used correctly. You can make a nice daily paycheck in a nice quiet way. Only $6.00.

23. HOW TO WIN AT VIDEO BLACKJACK . . .

Beating Blackjack slot machines will give you the best play every time. This book contains the best charts you need to beat just about every blackjack machine made. Every combination of cards is covered. Stop guessing and start winning. Only $6.00.

24. STRATEGY BLACKJACK CARD . . .

This little helper fits right in your wallet and is a big help when the cards have got you sweating. It is color-coded for easy reading and fast relief. It has 1 side for 1 & 2 decks and the 2nd side for multi-decks. This is a must for you Blackjack players. $3.00.

25. BLACKJACK . . . HOW TO PLAY AND WIN
LIKE AN EXPERT . . .

You will be a consistent winner when you have finished this book. No "fluff" here, you get to know the rules, betting system, an amazing, new easy counting system, basic strategy, how to manage your bankroll. With this book as your guide, you can go into any casino and play YOUR game instead of their game. $6.

26. MAGIC KIT . . . Learn Magic with the
Secret Invention . . .

EASY TO DO MAGIC! A book with over 25 easy to do magic tricks. Make a lit cigarette disappear into thin air, change a dollar bill into $.35, make salt disappear and then reappear in your hand, burst a balloon and see it restored. Props and Secret Invention included. Only $9.95.

THE FREE BONUS OFFER DOES NOT APPLY TO OUR NO CARD COUNTING, MAGIC KIT, & OR OUR COMPUTER SOFTWARE.

27. HOT DICE . . .

This book not only contains tested and proven results of thousands of hours of playing dice. It goes one step beyond and offers you the philosophy of how to develop and how to maintain a winning attitude. Just $6.

28. STUN GUN . . .

Protect yourself from muggers and rapists. Take self defense seriously. Only $39.95. Please add $5 for shipping and handling.

29. STUN GUN KEY CHAIN . . .
Another method of protecting yourself. This key chain has an electric shock stun effect. Only $39.95. Please add $5 for shipping and handling.

30. 25 DIFFERENT WAYS TO WAGER AT GOLF
AND WIN . . .
Another book written by Jimmy K. This book is filled with humor and good advice on wagering at golf. Only $4.

31. LAS VEGAS SECRETS . . .
This book contains ideas on what to do in Las Vegas if your spouse doesn't gamble or if you bring the kids. Learn all the ins and outs of things to do in Las Vegas. Only $5.

32. LAUGHLIN INSIDER . . .
An in-depth report on a gaming boomtown. Real estate, shops, and services, in charge jobs, recreation. Only $4.

33. WINNING SECRETS OF A
POKER MASTER . . .
You'll learn the art of bluffing, money systems, opening, betting. All sorts of poker variations are discussed along with strategies and rules for assessing your opponents. $6.

FROM GAMING BOOKS INTERNATIONAL
COMPUTER SOFTWARE DEPARTMENT
Our Gaming Software allows you to play a number of casino games on your home computer. The program plays just like the real thing and includes statistical analysis which allows you to determine the best playing strategy for any hand. It is currently available for the IBM or IBM compatible.

Computers, a monitor and keyboard are all that is required. No specialized peripherals necessary to enjoy these games.

34. COMPUTER BLACKJACK . . .
This booklet contains a software disk that you can use in your own computer at home. It is IBM or IBM compatible. Learn the tricks of the trade in the comfort of your home. Only $29.95.

35. COMPUTER KENO . . .
Try your favorite Keno Ticket on Computer Keno. Play the same ticket or a multiple of tickets. This is also IBM or IBM compatible. Over 200 games an hour. A fun game. You will enjoy this and you can play in your home. Only $29.95.

36. COMPUTER VIDEO POKER . . .
Available for the IBM or IBM compatible, and Commodore computers. Now you can learn the secrets of Video Poker in your own home. Only $29.95.

37. COMPUTER CRAPS . . .
   IBM compatible, learn to play the tables while at home. Try your own system or ours. It's a must for you crapshooters. Only $29.95.

PLEASE DON'T FORGET ABOUT OUR **"PLAYING TO WIN"** SERIES. A MUST FOR EVERY GAMBLER'S BOOKSHELF! WE PAY ALL POSTAGE, HANDLING, FREIGHT, TAX, LICENSE, INSURANCE, TRANSPORTATION AND DELIVERY, TO OR NEAR YOUR HOME WITHIN THE UNITED STATES. SUCH A DEAL!!! JUST $3.50

BLACKJACK	3.50	SLOTS	3.50
CRAPS	3.50	ROULETTE	3.50
POKER	3.50	BACCARAT	3.50
KENO	3.50	VIDEO POKER	3.50
HORSE RACING	3.50	SPORTS BETTING	3.50

CRAP SYSTEM – Try your crap system on over 3000 rolls of the dice. These rolls are actually recorded on special designed work sheets, so you can try your system before going to the tables. $9.95

BLACKJACK SYSTEM – Try your blackjack system on over 5000 hands. Actual played and recorded at the Las Vegas Blackjack tables. Try your system on these special designed work sheets before trying the blackjack table.
                                                           $9.95

FOR CREDIT CARD ORDERS OR COD PLEASE CONTACT:

GAMING BOOKS INTERNATIONAL
1512 E. FREMONT
LAS VEGAS, NEVADA 89101
(702) 477-7771